Afterlife

What Will It Be Like?

Warren Henderson

Afterlife – What Will It Be Like?
By Warren Henderson
Copyright © 2011

Published by Warren A. Henderson
3769 Indiana Road
Pomona, KS 66076

Cover Design by Ben Bredaweg

ISBN 978-0-9795387-8-0

ORDERING INFORMATION:
Case quantities of *Afterlife* may be purchased for $1.25/book through Gospel Folio Press. Individual copies may be obtained from Gospel Folio Press or various internet book-retailers.

Gospel Folio Press
Phone: 1-800-952-2382
Website: order@gospelfolio.com

Printed in the United States of America

Table of Contents

Other Books by the Author

Your Home the Birthing Place of Heaven
Glories Seen & Unseen
Seeds of Destiny – A Devotional Study of Genesis
Mind Frames – Where Life's Battle Is Won Or Lost
Behold the Saviour
Be Angry and Sin Not
Hallowed Be Thy Name – Revering Christ in a Casual World
The Fruitful Vine – Celebrating Biblical Womanhood
The Fruitful Bough – Affirming Biblical Manhood
The Olive Plants – Raising Spiritual Children
In Search of God – A Quest for Truth
Hiding God – The Ambition of World Religion
The Bible: Myth or Divine Truth?
Exploring the Pauline Epistles
Out of Egypt – A Devotional Study of Exodus
Answer the Call – Finding Life's Purpose
Overcoming Your Bully
Passing the Torch – Mentoring the Next Generation

Preface

We often speak of the distance between two objects in respect to the time required to journey between them. For example, the closest star to us, besides our own Sun, of course, is the faint, red dwarf star called Proxima Centauri. This star is just 4.2 light-years away. Alpha Centauri is another star which is also about 4.2 light-years away. A light-year is a measurement used to describe how far light travels in one year, which is approximately six trillion miles. Meaning the light that we see from these stars traveled about 1,500 days to reach us. The use of time as a measurement of distance is only possible because we understand that the speed of light is consistent at 186,282 miles per second.

A bit closer to home, we might use time to express a distance by saying something like, "I live fifty minutes from here," referring to the distance that one travels in an automobile after fifty minutes of driving. Yet, if we had to walk that same distance, we would refer to the same trip as being incredibly long. Although the distance traveled is unchanged, our perspective of the trip itself depends on the mode of transportation. In a car, our regard for the distance home is minimal, as it requires nearly no personal effort to traverse. Perhaps that is why many people ignore the matter of death – it is a high speed corridor into the unknown which does not require any personal effort to get there. But the question we should really be contemplating is: if this casual attitude about death is reasonable given that each of us is only one sigh away from venturing into the afterlife? Shouldn't we think about our own demise, and prepare for it and what follows, if it is possible to do so?

Empirical evidence indicates that, statistically speaking, one out of one dies – there is no natural means of avoiding death. All physical life on earth must die – nature teaches us that I must die and so must you. This means that one of us will be the next one to go. But where will we go after death, if anywhere at all? Is there a divine being or an intelligence that oversees this important matter? Is there life after death and, if so, what does that consist of? How can we be sure of such things? These are important questions that require careful contemplation and personal reflection.

Wise men throughout human history have contemplated such questions without achieving sound conclusions. For example, Tzekung once asked Confucius: "Do dead men know what is going on, or do they not?" Confucius answered: "If I were to say that dead men know what's going on I am afraid all of the filial sons and grandsons would inconvenience the living in order to accommodate the dead. But if I were to say that dead men don't know what's going on. I am afraid that unfilial offspring would just leave their dead unburied. Now, Son, if you wish to know whether or not dead men know, wait until you die and you will know soon enough!"[1] As demonstrated by Confucius's answer, humanism cannot conclusively answer questions pertaining to the afterlife. If the basis for reasoning death-related questions is solely based on observations in life, then obviously afterlife questions will go unanswered, as that realm, if it does exist, would not be governed by natural law.

It is my deepest conviction that we can know, and with certainty, what we will be and where we will be after death. Furthermore, we need not fear death, if we have properly prepared for eternity now. If you have ever wondered: "What happens when someone dies?" "Is there a spiritual realm of bliss and peace in the afterlife?" "Is there a place that wicked people will be judged?" "What will I be like after death?" "Will I recognize loved ones after I die?" please read on – life is too brief not to have such questions answered.

The Basis of Understanding

What is real? What is truth? What is the meaning of Life? These are perhaps bizarre questions to some, but at the heart of these inquiries is the basis for how each one of us will interpret life. What an individual believes to be ultimate truth will define his or her ideology for relating to all of life's issues.

Human reasoning is vitally important to finding answers to life's most crucial questions. Thankfully, absolute truth cannot contradict itself. That which is not found consistently accurate cannot be true. It is understood that scientific perception of absolute truth is imperfect, for science is a never-ending process which refines our understanding of what ultimate reality is. On this fact, Albert Einstein once remarked, "One thing I have learned in a long life – that all our science, measured against reality, is primitive and childlike."[1] Science is certainly a viable path to what is observably true or conditionally true, but imperfections in the measurement, interpretation, and evaluation of data ensure that a scientific truth is only truth within certain ranges – a statistically valid interpretation of ultimate truth.

Consequently, if man wants to know the truth concerning the subject of afterlife, he is going to have to look beyond science and fabricated religion for answers. My apologetics *In Search of God* and *The Bible: Myth or Divine Truth?* provide empirical evidence to verify that the Bible is uniformly true and consistently accurate with scientific findings. Certainly there are many things in the Bible which cannot be proven true, but there is no evidence to suggest that the Bible is not true; rather, there is much internal and external evidence that validates the biblical narrative as true. Significant archaeological findings and evidence from other fields of science substantiate this statement.

Unlike "holy books" from various world religions, God's Word, the Bible, has and will stand the test of time; it is absolute and immutable. There is no other book on the planet with its authenticity, uniform composition, and prophetic content.

If this assertion is true, it stands to reason that the Bible is an explicit expression of absolute truth to mankind. Reason then dictates that man should strive to learn of its message and heed its warning. It is therefore stated at the onset that the Bible will be the foundation in which we derive our basis of understanding to answer our questions pertaining to afterlife. The term *worldview* refers to any ideology, philosophy, theology, etc. which provides an intellectual framework for interpreting life, including the metaphysical properties associated with existing. For the reasons previously stated, I hold a monotheistic worldview with biblical Christianity at its core.

When it comes to the subject of afterlife, we should understand that *eternity is too long to be wrong*. It is my earnest belief that Biblical Christianity best answers afterlife questions and I would ask you to spend the next thirty minutes or so considering that possibility. The fact is that most of us will be dead a whole lot longer than we will be alive, so a few minutes spent contemplating this important subject now will be a good investment for eternity.

Biblical Christianity

As there is much confusion today about what "Christianity" actually is, we will begin by defining the term. *Biblical Christianity* is not an earthly institution, or a humanly-conspired organization, or a set of systematized teachings per se, but rather it is an opportunity to experience spiritual union with Jesus Christ. Christian author Josiah Strong put it this way: "Christianity is neither a creed nor a ceremony, but a life vitally connected with a loving Christ."[2] Oneness with Christ secures eternal life and affords the believer an opportunity to enjoy (as he or she yields to Christ) a life that is meaningful and pleasing to God (Luke 9:23-26).

The message of Jesus Christ ensures that a human relationship with God and a humanized religious zeal for God will never be reconciled – both are unique and separate approaches for seeking divine favor. Yet, this dichotomy is one of the hardest spiritual realities for man to comprehend and accept. While preaching on the streets of San Francisco nearly a century ago, Bible commentator Harry Ironside (1876-1951) reported that he was often interrupted by a common outburst such as this:

> "Look here, sir! There are hundreds of religions in this country, and the followers of each sect think theirs the only right one. How can poor, plain men like us find out what really is the truth?"

> We generally replied something like this: "Hundreds of religions, you say? That's strange; I've heard of only two."

> "Oh, but you surely know there are more than that?"

> "Not at all, sir, I find, I admit, many shades of difference in the opinions of those comprising the two great schools; but after all there are but two. The one covers all who expect salvation by doing; the other, all who have been saved by something done. So you see the whole question is very simple. Can you save yourself, or must you be saved by another? If you can be your own savior, you do not need my message. If you cannot, you may well listen to it."[3]

The main distinction between Christianity and all the religions of the world is that biblical Christianity teaches that man has a vital need to be saved from spiritual death by trusting in the Savior alone, whereas the world's religions pose a system of *doing* to merit salvation or to obtain an improved afterlife. Religion equips man with a "do it yourself" manual and workbook through which he may impress himself as to how well he is *doing* by completing religious exercises and checklists. Christianity, however, is not a *religion*; it is a *relationship* with Jesus Christ. Apart from Christ, there is no forgiveness of sins, no life, and no hope – this is the Christian message as revealed in the Bible.

> Religion is humans trying to work their way to God through good works. Christianity is God coming to men and women through Jesus Christ offering them a relationship with Himself.

> — Josh McDowell

Biblical *faith* is not blind belief as some skeptics claim. On the contrary, the Bible challenges its readers to test and reason out Scripture. *"Test all things; hold fast what is good"* (1 Thess. 5:21). This testing is not for the purpose of proving that Scripture is true, but to personally affirm that it is true. Paul complimented the Bereans because *"they received the word with all readiness of mind, and searched the Scriptures daily, whether those things were so"* (Acts 17:11, KJV).

Biblical Christianity has this distinction over the religious movements of the world; the reader is challenged to test the Scripture to validate in his or her own mind its truthfulness. Religion imposes propaganda without permitting an opportunity to validate truthfulness against itself and available evidence. God knows man will only faithfully live out that which he has first proven to be true. The fear and scare tactics of the world's religions effectively strangle the heart from ever exercising love in the truth.

When it comes to embracing divine truth, there is no middle ground – only our ignorance, cowardice, and complacency permit us to live a lackadaisical and sanctimonious existence apart from God. Christian apologist C. S. Lewis put it this way: "Christianity, if false, is of no importance, and, if true, of infinite importance. The one thing it cannot be is moderately important."[4] It is only by knowing and trusting absolute truth, God's revealed truth in Christ, that one's entrance into heaven is ensured: *Jesus said to him, "I am the way, the truth, and the life. No one comes to the Father except through Me"* (John 14:6).

Whether the reader is a Christian or not, it is important to have an accurate biblical view of what Christianity actually is. The cults and humanized Christianity have caused much distortion of this truth and the reader is encouraged to understand the difference between biblical Christianity and what world religion says that it is.

Facing Death

About the year 125 AD a Greek by the name of Aristeides was writing to one of his friends about the new religion, Christianity. He was trying to explain the reasons for its extraordinary success. Here is a sentence from one of his letters: "If any righteous man among the Christians passes from this world, they rejoice and offer thanks to God, and they escort his body with songs and thanksgiving as if he were setting out from one place to another nearby."[1] Why is it that these Christians and millions more down through the centuries have faced death with confidence? The short answer is that they had the hope of a bodily resurrection and that they would spend eternity with the Lord Jesus Christ. Christians who follow the teachings of Christ do not take up arms in religious causes, but rather seek to live for Christ and willingly suffer the consequences of doing so. They understand that the earth is a temporary abode which God uses to prepare them for heaven. Peter put the matter this way:

> For this is commendable, if because of conscience toward God one endures grief, suffering wrongfully. For what credit is it if, when you are beaten for your faults, you take it patiently? But when you do good and suffer, if you take it patiently, this is commendable before God. For to this you were called, because Christ also suffered for us, leaving us an example, that you should follow His steps (1 Pet. 2:19-21).

Peter, himself facing martyrdom, sought to encourage others to patiently endure persecution and follow the Lord's example of suffering for righteousness' sake (1 Pet. 1:12-15, 20-21). This is one of the pleasing distinctions of true Christianity over the major monotheistic world religions (excluding Judaism) - its Founder and His followers did not beset a path of violence in the

11

conversion of others to Christianity. On the contrary, over the centuries a faithful remnant of true Christians have held to the teachings of Christ, though led like sheep to the slaughter for their faith. *Foxe's Book of Martyrs* and *The Pilgrim Church* by E. H. Broadbent are excellent historical resources that document this fact.

A religion based on hate will be sustained by fear and the drive for self-preservation, but that which is forged in love will be propagated by sacrificial service. This is the testimony of true Christians for the last two thousand years, beginning with the original followers of Christ. What they believed was lived out in selfless sacrifice even unto their death. Being assured of the truth, they did not defend themselves from tyranny, mockery, and martyrdom. The assurance of God's Word resulted in hope for the future and joy while bearing tremendous pain and suffering. They knew if they died that they would be with the Lord (2 Cor. 5:8), and that in a future day they would experience a bodily resurrection (1 Thess. 4:13).

Before the Lord Jesus went to Calvary to willingly suffer for humanity's sins, He promised His disciples that after He prepared a place for them in heaven He would come back for them (John 14:1-3). Obviously, our earthly bodies, which are prone to sin, are not fit for heaven – they need to be supernaturally changed, and resurrection accomplishes just that. Not only did the disciples have the Lord's promise of being with Him in heaven, they personally saw Him after He was raised from the dead. This had a profound impact on them – seeing and speaking with their resurrected Savior was an experience they never got over.

Facing Death with Hope

How did those early disciples emphatically demonstrate that they had witnessed the resurrection of their Lord? They willingly laid down their lives to show love and obedience to their Savior – men do not peacefully die for a lie – these people were fully convinced of the claims of Christ Jesus. Peter, Andrew, James (son of Alphaeus), Philip, Simon, and Bartholomew were crucified in various ways. Matthew and James (the son of Zebedee) were slain by the sword; Thaddaeus was struck by many arrows;

Thomas was thrust through with a spear, and James (the half-brother of Jesus) was cast over the temple wall and, after plummeting to the ground, was finished off by stoning. John Mark bled to death after being tied to a chariot and dragged through the streets of Alexandria. John was the only disciple not to experience martyrdom; his latter years were spent in exile on the Isle of Patmos as a prisoner. It is true that some people are conned into dying for religious causes, but the disciples would not have died for a resurrection hoax they themselves had concocted; rather, they died for what they knew to be true. Sane men don't willingly die for what they know is a lie.

History records that Aegeas crucified Andrew, Peter's brother, for his faith in Christ. Seeing his cross before him, Andrew bravely spoke, "O cross, most welcome and longed for! With a willing mind, joyfully and desirously, I come to thee, being the scholar of Him which did hang on thee: because I have always been thy lover, and have coveted to embrace thee."[2] Why would Andrew approach his cross with joy? He had watched the Lord approach His cross in the same manner. During the deepest trials of life, it is possible to have present joy in God's future promises. Each of the Lord's disciples faced death with the same hope and endured tremendous suffering for the joy set before them.

Often when you ask someone if they are going to heaven (which most people consider to be an eternal place of bliss), he or she will respond by saying, "I hope so." Yet, it was not a "hope so" supposition which prompted the disciples to lay down their lives; it was a "know so" reality. But how could they have such confidence in eternal matters? The answer to this question can be found in Peter's reply to the Lord after He asked him if he would cease to follow Him after supposed followers were offended at Christ's teachings. Peter declared, *"Lord, to whom shall we go? You have the words of eternal life. Also we have come to believe and know that You are the Christ, the Son of the living God"* (John 6:68-69). The writer of Hebrews explains what this faith is: *"Now faith is the substance of things hoped for, the evidence of things not seen"* (Heb 11:1-2); this is why the disciples could face death with confidence; they knew who Christ was and trusted Him explicitly. The Lord had told them,

"Most assuredly, I say to you, he who believes in Me has everlasting life" (John 6:47). They chose to believe what the Lord said was true; thus, their faith, rooted in divine truth, produced hope! Hope is having present joy in future promises and it can only be obtained through exercising faith in the Word of God.

The disciples knew beyond any shadow of doubt that Jesus Christ was who He proclaimed to be. The miracles that He performed provided evidence to this truth and they had witnessed the greatest of all miracles – resurrection from the dead. To deny such things would be ludicrous and, in effect, call Jesus Christ a liar! There is no logical middle ground on this matter; as Thomas Aquinas surmised centuries ago, "Christ was either liar, lunatic, or Lord!"[3] So which is it? Christ must be Lord of all, or not Lord at all. Anything less than complete trust in Christ and His Word will be shown through one's anxiety about the future and the fear of death. The writer of Hebrews acknowledges that Christ has released *"those who through fear of death were all their lifetime subject to bondage"* (Heb. 2:15). Although the dying part is no fun, death itself is a mere doorway into the spiritual realm; for Christians, death is a door leading into the presence of Christ. The Lord Jesus, at the right hand of His Father, stood up to receive Stephen, the first martyr of the Church, into heaven (Acts 7:54-60). Dear reader, He promises to receive you also, if you will only trust in Him alone for salvation!

Facing Death Alone

Leaving the biblical viewpoint of death for a moment, let us consider a secular perspective. Dr. Maurice Rawlings is a world expert on near-death experiences, and the author of three books on the subject. Dr. Rawlings was the former Clinical Assistant Professor of Medicine for the University of Tennessee at Chattanooga and also the former personal physician at the Pentagon for the Joint Chiefs of Staff. Dr. Rawlings and his colleagues are constantly treating emergency patients, many of whom have had near-death experiences. A study of these cases was reported in the March 1985 issue of Omni magazine. Dr. Rawlings reported, "It is no longer unusual to hear about people who have almost died who speak of seeing a bright light, lush green meadows, rows of smiling relatives and experiencing a deep sense of peace." His studies included much information obtained from his patients by interviewing them immediately following resuscitation (while they are very much in touch with their experience). Dr. Rawlings says that nearly fifty percent of the 300 people that he has interviewed have reported lakes of fire, devil-like figures and other sights reflecting the darkness of hell. Rawlings also reported that these people later changed their story because they didn't want to admit where they had been, not even to their families. "Just listening to these patients has changed my whole life," claims Dr. Rawlings. "There is a life after death, and if I don't know where I'm going, it's not safe to die."[4]

That profound sentiment would characterize the last words of Charles IX, who ordered the massacre of Protestants on the eve of St. Bartholomew's Day; he muttered: "What blood! What murders! I know not where I am. How will all this end? What shall I do? I am lost forever. I know it."[5] It was reported that just before dying his soul was in such anguish that his perspiration was mixed with blood.[6] An atheist writer by the name of Thomas Paine at the end of his life said, "I would give worlds if I had them, that *The Age of Reason* had never been published. O Lord, help me! Christ, help me! No, don't leave; stay with me! Send even a child to stay with me; for I am on the edge of Hell here alone. If ever the Devil had an agent, I have been that one."[7]

A failing Bertrand Russell, a twentieth century British mathematician and philosopher, one who openly and frequently opposed the Christian faith, said the following just before he died, "Philosophy has proven a washout for me."[8] As Caesar Borgia came to the end of his life, he declared, "While I lived, I provided for everything but death; now I must die, and AM UNPREPARED TO DIE."[9] It has been said the atheists die hard and the above testimonies would seem to indicate that fact is true. Anxiety, guilt, and fear were prevalent just before their spirits wrenched themselves free of their bodies.

How Do You Face Death?

In contrast with the above testimonies, Christians often have favorable experiences as they pass into eternity. For example, Thomas Edison, a scientific genius and a Christian, just moments before his death said to his wife and doctor, "It is beautiful over there."[10] Edison was a man of science, a pursuer of truth before all else. Would he have made such a statement, if he had not believed it to be true? When the great scientist Michael Faraday was dying, some journalists questioned him as to his speculations for a life after death. "Speculations!" said he, "I know nothing about speculations. I'm resting on certainties. 'I know that my Redeemer lives,' and because He lives, I shall live also."[11]

Frances Havergal, the Christian hymn writer, spent much time in God's Word. On the last day of her life, she asked a friend to read to her the 42nd chapter of Isaiah. When the friend read the sixth verse: *"I the Lord have called thee in righteousness, and will hold thine hand, and will keep thee,"* Miss Havergal stopped her. She whispered, "Called—held—kept. I can go home on that!" And a few moments later she did.[12]

During World War II, a fellow prisoner of Dietrich Bonhoeffer wrote: "Sunday, April 8, 1945, Pastor Bonhoeffer held a little service which reached the hearts of all. He had hardly finished his prayer, when the door opened. Two evil-looking soldiers came in and barked: 'Prisoner Bonhoeffer, come with us!' The words meant only one thing, the scaffold. As he bid his fellow prisoners good-bye, he said, 'For me this is the beginning of a new life, eternal life.'"[13] A few minutes later, Dietrich Bonhoeffer was in the presence of the Lord.

It is faith in God's Word alone that allows believers to face death with the same enthusiasm and hope as they embrace life. Death is simply a doorway into the afterlife; it is not the door itself that should concern us, but what lies behind it. What one knows to be beyond the door will drastically influence his or her willingness to walk through it! If you fear death, it is most likely because you are not convinced of what is beyond death's door or because you know, but don't want to do anything about it now. Are you afraid of what lies beyond death? Do you have hope for your tomorrow, when your last yesterday might be today?

Three Deaths and One Life

Several types of death are spoken of in Scripture, but there are three deaths, or literally, "separations," that are most significant to all mankind. We are all born *spiritually dead*; that is, we are spiritually separated from God. Then, when *physical death* occurs, our soul and spirit separate from our body. If physical death occurs while a person is still spiritually dead, *eternal death* (judgment in hell) is assured. Hebrews 9:27 proclaims, *"It is appointed unto men once to die, but after this the judgment."* The only exception to the above is that perhaps God will demonstrate His grace by applying the blood of Christ to the souls of those who died in the womb or early in life, before they understood the moral law within them and God's solution to their sin problem (2 Sam. 12:23). God calls these young ones "innocent" (Jer. 19:4). But as adults and older children, the unsaved are just one heartbeat, one breath away from sealing an eternal destiny of woe.

When Death Began

God had informed Adam shortly after his creation, *"Of every tree of the garden you may freely eat, but of the tree of the knowledge of good and evil you shall not eat, for in the day that you eat of it you shall surely die"* (Gen. 2:16-17). Life was wonderful in Eden until that horrible day that changed the course of humanity forever. Satan solicited Eve to eat the forbidden fruit so that she might be like God. Eve, then Adam, chose to believe the "father of lies" instead of God. The same satanic deception and desire for knowledge presently blinds many from heeding the truth that would liberate their souls from the bondage of sin.

After Adam and his wife disobeyed God and ate of the forbidden tree, their fellowship with God was instantly severed. They now felt uneasy with God and even tried to hide from His presence. Billows of guilt and waves of shame relentlessly pounded their awakened conscience. The anguish of impending judgment swept over them like a flood. God judged them and thrust them out of the garden to struggle for survival on a cursed planet. Instead of significance, they felt rejection. Gone too was their security; they were now on their own, having to rely on their own strength and self-control to live. In a brief moment their secure and significant communion with God was forfeited. Now feelings of rejection, shame, and helplessness overwhelmed them. The immensity of that moment for our first parents was staggering – they now would live without God's communion.

Unlike other creatures, when God created Adam, He breathed into him an eternal spirit, which gave Adam consciousness of God (Gen. 2:7; Job 27:3, 32:8). As descendents of Adam, this spirit resides in us also and awakens our minds to the reality of God's existence and that there is life after death. During a nighttime stroll, man will invariably gaze heavenward, and while beholding the starry host upon a canopy of blackness, a voice deep within him whispers, "There is Someone out there – there is a God." The Psalmist writes, *"You will light my lamp; the Lord my God will enlighten my darkness"* (Ps. 18:28). God is seeking the rebel and calling him back to Himself. God's Spirit pleads through our own human spirit to draw near and be restored to our Creator. The Lord Jesus said that it is impossible for man to worship God except through his spirit and in divine truth; this necessitates trusting the truth of Christ's message in order to be spiritually restored to God (John 4:24).

Our human spirit desperately needs God and communion with Him to be satisfied. Being impoverished of two senses, a blind and deaf Helen Keller acknowledged eloquently what her spirit cried out from within, "I believe in the immortality of the soul because I have within me immortal longings."[1] It is only through man's spirit that worship can be rendered to God (Phil. 3:3). Consequently, at the spirit level of man resides his most intense need – to be one with his Creator. Many will try to fill this void with religiosity, others with momentary thrills that satisfy base lusts (e.g. drugs, amusements, unlawful sex); others, with more sophisticated fascinations (e.g. fame, power, intellect, and wealth). What temporal stimulus could ever satisfy man's deepest spiritual need to be one with his Creator? None. My spirit has a deep longing that only God can satisfy.

Peter, speaking of Jesus Christ, said, *"Nor is there salvation in any other, for there is no other name under heaven given among men by which we must be saved"* (Acts 4:12). To alleviate any confusion about what the true gospel message actually is, the Lord Jesus Christ personally conveyed it to Paul, who wrote: *"For I delivered to you first of all that which I also received: that Christ died for our sins according to the Scriptures, and that He was buried, and that He rose again the third day according to the Scriptures"* (1 Cor 15:3-4). So if by faith, one believes and receives Christ for the forgiveness of his or her sins, he or she is then born again (speaking of spiritual birth, see John 3:3; 1 Pet. 1:23). Believing any other gospel than this brings eternal damnation (Gal. 1:6-9).

The prophet Isaiah describes humanity as sheep which go their own way and become lost: *"All we like sheep have gone astray; we have turned, every one, to his own way"* (Isa. 53:6). Praise be to God that He comes seeking and calling to bring us back to Himself! What should be our response? Isaiah says, *"Seek the Lord while He may be found, call upon Him while He is near* (Isa. 55:6). But, to seek the Lord one must repent (turn from going his or her own way and agree with God about the matter of sin). Then, a seeking Savior and a seeking sinner will find each other. Fortunately for us, God is seeking us out through the finished work of Christ and by the drawing ministry of the Holy Spirit. God's offer for salvation is to whomsoever will respond (Matt. 11:28-30), for God is *"not willing that any should perish but that all should come to repentance"* (2 Pet. 3:9).

When Death Ends

The only way to personally beat death is to receive eternal life in Christ; while those in Christ may experience physical death, they will never experience spiritual death. While speaking to Martha, the Lord affirmed, *"I am the resurrection and the life. He who believes in Me, though he may die, he shall live. And whoever lives and believes in Me shall never die. Do you believe this?"* (John 11:25-26). The Lord Jesus likened the receiving of His life to being born again. He told an inquiring Pharisee named Nicodemus, *"Most assuredly, I say to you, unless one is born again, he cannot see the kingdom of God"* (John 3:3). In other words, no one can make it to heaven without receiving spiritual life in Christ. John explained that most rejected Jesus Christ as their Savior, but some did trust in him. For those who did, John says that they were born again and became God's spiritual children: *"But as many as received Him, to them He gave the right to become children of God, to those who believe in His name: who were born, not of blood, nor of the will of the flesh, nor of the will of man, but of God"* (John 1:12-13). So, without being born again (receiving Christ's life) one cannot become a child of God, and one cannot be born again without trusting the Lord Jesus Christ for salvation. In this way, the Christian can enjoy the re-surrection life of Christ now (Phil. 3:10) and have the hope of bodily resurrection into His presence later (1 Cor. 15:51-52).

Paul understood that the resurrection of the dead was more than just an "I hope so" crutch to get the believer through tough times; it was a essential part of the believer's salvation. He stated that if there was no resurrection of the dead, *"then also those who have fallen asleep in Christ have perished. If in this life only we have hope in Christ, we are of all men the most pitiable"* (1 Cor. 15:18-19). Without resurrection there is no salvation! *"For if the dead do not rise, then Christ is not risen. And if Christ is not risen, your faith is futile; you are still in your sins!"* (1 Cor. 15:16-17). Why would Paul place such importance on the resur-rection of Christ, even to say that if He had not been raised, that though we believed on Him we would still be dead in our sins?

Picture yourself visiting a terminally ill friend in a hospital. While you are talking to your friend, she gets drowsy, closes her eyes, stops breathing, and a few moments later quietly passes into eternity. If you could raise your friend from the dead would she be any better off? No, she has a deadly disease and would just die again. If you could somehow instantly heal her disease would she be any better off? No, she would just be a healthy dead person. Your friend needs both life and to be healed from her disease. The Lord Jesus dealt with the deadly disease called sin at Calvary, and because He was raised from the dead, believers cannot only be forgiven of their sins, but they in Him receive His life. The Lord Jesus gave up His life that we might live His life out now. This is why the Lord could say, *"My sheep hear My voice, and I know them, and they follow Me. And I give them eternal life, and they shall never perish; neither shall anyone snatch them out of My hand"* (John 10:27-28). In Christ there is eternal life; outside Christ there is only death!

God's personal offer to be one with Him is rescinded when physical death occurs. The Lord's teaching found in Luke 16 confirms that if someone dies apart from trusting God for salvation, the spiritual essence of that person will await final judgment in a place of torment called Hades. The Lord explains that there was a certain rich man who died and was taken by angels to Hades and being in torment begged Abraham, who was residing in paradise, to send a poor beggar named Lazarus to his aid. The Lord Jesus describes the scene and the dialogue which took place:

> *And being in torments in Hades, he lifted up his eyes and saw Abraham afar off, and Lazarus in his bosom. Then he cried and said, "Father Abraham, have mercy on me, and send Lazarus that he may dip the tip of his finger in water and cool my tongue; for I am tormented in this flame." But Abraham said, "Son, remember that in your lifetime you received your good things, and likewise Lazarus evil things; but now he is comforted and you are tormented. And besides all this, between us and you there is a great gulf fixed, so that those who want to pass from here to you cannot, nor can those from there pass to us." Then he said, "I beg you therefore, father, that you would send him to my father's house, for I have five brothers, that he may testify to them, lest they also come to this place of torment." Abraham said to him, 'They have Moses and the prophets; let them hear them"* (Luke 16: 22-29).

Because the rich man only requested one drop of water to cool his tongue, it is likely he knew his chances of obtaining any relief from his torment was impossible – a matter Abraham later affirmed. In fact, Abraham states there was a barrier between their realms of habitation to ensure that the wicked remain in their prison. Notice that these disembodied souls are completely conscious of their surroundings and are able to communicate, meaning that there is no such thing as *soul sleep* after death (as some sects teach), nor does the human soul cease to exist after death (a position that most cults hold to).

The rich man seeing his wretched state became an instant evangelist – he did not want other family members to die and end up with him in Hades. He pleaded with Abraham that Lazarus return to the physical realm to warn his brothers about the terrible place to where he had gone. Abraham explained that true faith is not based on sight, and even if his brothers witnessed someone returning from the dead to warn them, they would not believe in the miracle of resurrection (Luke 16:30-32). Abraham told the rich man that his living family members had the Word of God, which was spoken by Moses and the prophets, and that they needed nothing else to know what God expected of them. The same is true today; when individuals choose to trust God's Word alone for salvation they need not fear ever going to Hades and then the Lake of Fire. Paul adamantly states that those in Christ have salvation and will never experience divine wrath:

> *But God demonstrates His own love toward us, in that while we were still sinners, Christ died for us. Much more then, having now been justified by His blood, we shall be saved from wrath through Him.* (Rom. 5:8-9).

Why could Paul be so sure that believers would never suffer God's judicial wrath? Because God would be unjust to punish Christians again for offenses He had already punished His Son for on their behalf. To do so would mean that Christ did not satisfy God's need of justice at Calvary. But Paul explains that complete propitiation was obtained through the sufferings of Christ for all human sin (Rom. 3:25; 1 John 2:2). Christ experienced death for everyone, so that we could have an opportunity to escape eternal death (Heb. 2:9). But, as the rich man found out, God's offer to be saved has limitations, and we are just one breath away from personally understanding what those are.

Two Resurrections

It is quite possible that Job is the oldest book in our Bibles, and ironically, it is the first to speak of resurrection. Scripture declares that Job *"was blameless and upright, and one that feared God, and shunned evil"* (Job 1:1). He was an honorable man who suffered greatly for the glory of God and for personal refinement. Even after the loss of all his wealth, his children, and his health, Job would not blaspheme God, but instead anticipated being with Him in the afterlife:

> *For I know that my Redeemer lives, and He shall stand at last on the earth; and after my skin is destroyed, this I know, that in my flesh I shall see God, whom I shall see for myself, and my eyes shall behold, and not another. How my heart yearns within me!* (Job 19:25-27).

Even if God took Job's life, he understood that he would be resurrected in a future day and that he would dwell with his Redeemer. Though Job suffered greatly, God did restore and bless him later in his life (Job 42). What was his hope during those difficult days? He knew that his resurrected body would not be covered with sores, but would fully prepare him to be with his God.

Natural law governs us while we sojourn on earth, but that is not true in the spiritual realm of the afterlife. Whether one spends eternity in heaven or in hell, everyone one will undergo a spiritual resurrection. This ensures that all individuals will have a body suited for their final destination. The Lord Jesus taught that He, as the Son of God, created all life and that all life was in Him (John 1:3-4). He also stated that at His command all the deceased would be resurrected (i.e. every disembodied soul would be joined to an immortal body that can never die):

> *Most assuredly, I say to you, he who hears My word and believes in Him who sent Me has everlasting life, and shall not come into judgment, but has passed from death into life. Most assuredly, I say to you, the hour is coming, and now is, when the dead will hear the voice of the Son of God; and those who hear will live. For as the Father has life in Himself, so He has granted the Son to have life in Himself, and has given Him authority to execute judgment also, because He is the Son of Man. Do not marvel at this; for the hour is coming in which all who are in the graves will hear His voice and come forth – those who have done good, to the resurrection of life, and those who have done evil, to the resurrection of condemnation* (John 5:24-29).

From this passage we learn that there will be two types of resurrection: a resurrection of the just to enable eternal residence in heaven and a resurrection of the condemned to be punished for eternity in the Lake of Fire (Rev. 20:10, 15). The Lord Jesus has received authority from His Father to initiate both of these resurrections, but Scripture informs us that the first resurrection (i.e. of the just) occurs in several stages, while the resurrection of the condemned happens all at once.

Timing of the Resurrections

Though the resurrection of the condemned occurs all at once at the Great White Throne judgment (Rev. 20:11-15), the *resurrection of life*, also called the *first resurrection* (Rev. 20:5-6), occurs for the righteous at several distinct points in time prior to the Great White Throne judgment. The Eternal State, the everlasting reality of a new heaven and new earth without sin follows this final judgment. Time ceases to have meaning after this. Christ was raised from the dead three days after He gave His life as a ransom for humanity at Calvary. Though there had been six bodily resurrections recorded in the Bible previously, Christ was the first individual to experience glorification (to receive a glorified body which would be suitable for the dynamics of heaven). The number seven is used in the Bible to symbolize completeness and perfection and Christ, the seventh human raised from the dead, was the first to experience perfect resurrection; as Paul puts it, the Lord Jesus was *"the first fruits of the dead"* to appear before God in heaven (1 Cor. 15:20-23).

Shortly after Christ's resurrection, some deceased believers were also raised from the dead, probably as further validation of Christ's own resurrection. They either underwent a bodily resurrection (like Lazarus' resurrection recorded in John 12) or glorification (the same type of resurrection that Christ experienced) – Scripture does not specify which type. If this were only a bodily resurrection, those saints would have had to die a second time. It seems unlikely that God would have allowed these saints to enjoy fellowship with Christ in paradise and then put them back on the earth again to live a normal human existence in a sin-cursed world.

The next stage of the first resurrection will be when Christ returns for His Church. He will descend into the clouds and all true believers (both those who have died and also those still alive) will be quickly caught up from the earth to experience glorification (1 Thess. 4:13-18; 1 Cor. 15:51-52). At that moment, all Christians (and perhaps Old Testament saints as well, per Heb. 11:39-40) will receive the same kind of perfect body that the Lord did after His resurrection (Phil. 3:21; 1 Jn. 3:2). This spectacular event ends the Church Age and will be followed by a devastating period on earth called the Tribulation.

After all true Christians (i.e. those who had been born again and are indwelt by God) have been removed from the earth, the Antichrist will be allowed to rule the world for seven years (2 Thess. 2:4-7; Daniel 9:27). God will pour out great wrath upon the earth at this time and Satan will attempt to gain as many followers as possible and slaughter those who will not take his mark and pledge allegiance to the Antichrist (Rev. 12:12, 13:11-18). The holocaust of life during this time will be horrendous; the Lord Jesus said that if He should tarry longer than the appointed time for His return to the earth, that humanity would be wiped out (Matt. 24:21-22). Considering the twenty-one specific divine judgments which occur at this time (Rev. 6 – 17), the Battle of Gog and Magog (Ezek. 38 & 39), the chastening of Israel (Rom. 9:27), and the Battle of Armageddon (Rev. 19), it is quite conceivable that seventy-five percent of the world population will die during this epoch. Two-thirds of all Jews will be murdered during the Tribulation Period (Zech. 13:7-8), but God will protect a remnant of His covenant people from the Antichrist (Rev. 12:13-17) in order to fulfill remaining promises to Abraham and David (Gen. 15:18-2; Ps. 89:3-4; Luke 1:32-33, 67-79).

The good news is that many will choose to be beheaded by the Antichrist (Rev. 20:4) rather than take his mark of identification and worship him (Rev. 7:9-14). Those who heard the gospel message of Jesus Christ during the Church Age, will not be given the opportunity to receive salvation during the Tribulation Period – they will take *"the mark of the beast"* and follow him into destruction (2 Thess. 2:10-12). Because they rejected God's Son's offer of salvation and opted instead to pursue pleasure in unrighteousness, God will not allow them to understand the truth in order to be saved. On the other hand, those martyred for choosing to worship God rather than the Antichrist will experience the first resurrection at the end of the Tribulation Period (Rev. 20:4). This miraculous event coincides with Christ's physical return to the earth to destroy the Antichrist, to judge and remove wickedness from the earth, and to establish His earthly kingdom, which will last one thousand years (Rev. 20:4-6).

Revelation 20:1-8 informs us that Satan will be bound in the bottomless pit during Christ's reign on earth. However, at the end of that time he will be released to again to test man's resolve to follow God. Even after one thousand years of peace and prosperity, the devil will successfully deceive the nations of the earth to rebel against Christ. One might ask, "Why would God allow Satan to lead such a rebellion against His own Son? Why not just destroy Satan and be done with wickedness?" Unfortunately, wickedness would not expire with the end of Satan, for his rebel spirit entered into the world in Eden and intruded into humanity (1 Jn. 2:16). Death and rebellion have been passed down to every generation since that time (Rom. 5:12). Summarizing the state of the human heart, the prophet Jeremiah wrote, *"The heart is deceitful above all things, and desperately wicked; who can know it? I, the Lord, search the heart, I test the mind, even to give every man according to his ways, according to the fruit of his doings"* (Jer. 17:9-10). Before destroying Satan, God will allow him to test the human heart's fortitude for godliness, and find it lacking. While enjoying God's fellowship in a perfect environment, both the first man (Adam) and the last humans on earth before it is destroyed (Rev. 20:11, 21:1; 1 Pet. 3:10) are shown to be incapable of pleasing God when tempted to sin against Him.

Man, left to himself, will always go his own way; he will turn away from God (Isa. 53:6). God provided a righteous solution for human rebellion by judging His Son Jesus Christ in our place and giving those who would trust in Him eternal life. Those who will not trust in God's means of salvation in Christ will experience eternal death in hell. So, no matter when individuals live, no matter what dispensation of accountability is present when they lived, all the redeemed (those justified by faith) will experience the first resurrection and enter into the Eternal State, all others will receive resurrected bodies before being cast into the Lake of Fire. These are the only two types of eternal resurrections that the Bible identifies – one to everlasting life and one to everlasting torment and separation from God.

The Second and Final Resurrection

Satan's final rebellion will end when the earth is destroyed at the conclusion of Christ's Millennial Kingdom. At that time, God will judge the wicked and cast them into the Lake of Fire. This spiritual abode is often referred to as "hell," and was originally created for the purpose of punishing Satan and his fallen angels (Matt. 25:41). Before God creates a new heaven and earth, He will resurrect those who would not receive the truth of salvation by faith. God is a good record-keeper and is faithful to uphold His Word. A number of books will be opened at this divine trial to demonstrate that God is fully cognizant of sin and just in punishing the wicked for their sins. In fact, the wicked, knowing their own guilt, will not attempt to plead their case before Him (Ps. 64:1; Rom. 3:19). Consequently, all who are tried at the Great White Judgment are found guilty of violating God's perfect, righteous standard.

God's minimum requirement to enter into heaven is sinless perfection. Committing just one sin during one's entire life will prevent entrance into God's presence, that is, unless one has been declared righteous in Christ. Though the Christian is not sinless, he or she has a position of sinless perfection in Christ, and indeed, because of that union should sin less (Rom 6:1-4). As no one can undo one morally wrong act through the performance of many good ones, it is impossible to enter heaven by doing good works (Rom. 4:3-4; Eph. 2:8-9).

To believe that one is deserving of heaven through doing good deeds is an offensive notion to God, for that would mean that His judgment of His own Son on our behalf did not sufficiently satisfy His righteous demand for justice. This mindset means that individuals are really trusting in themselves and not in Christ alone for salvation. It is the erroneous message of world religion that you can improve your own spiritual essence or position through personal effort – essentially, you don't need a Savior. World religions says, "do, do, do," while biblical Christianity proclaims, "done, done, done." The former promotes personal effort for salvation, while the later acknowledges that only personal faith in a Savior can save. Accordingly, everyone resurrected to stand before God at the Great White Throne judgment will be found guilty and cast into the Lake of Fire (Rev. 20:11-15).

Resurrected Bodies

C. H. Spurgeon, the prince of preachers, once received a copy of Andrew Bonar's *Commentary on Leviticus*. It so blessed him that he returned the book to the author and requested the following favor: "Dr. Bonar, please place herein your autograph and your photograph." The book was returned to him with the following note from Dr. Bonar: "Dear Spurgeon, here is the book with my autograph and with my photograph. If you had been willing to wait a short season, you could have had a better likeness, for I shall be like Him; I shall see Him as He is (I Jn. 3:2)."[1] Dr. Bonar understood that there was a time coming that his appearance would be much more pleasant to the beholder. Why? Because after experiencing resurrection, believers will perfectly reflect the glory of Christ to all who behold them. Although yet appearing differently from each other, the outshining of God's glory will characterize all those in heaven.

So astonishing are the redeemed in heaven that John, who was caught up into heaven in the Spirit, fell down to worship fellow believers on two separate occasions (Rev. 19:10; 22:9). Both times the recipients of John's esteem abruptly admonished the apostle to stop and to worship God alone. John was the beloved disciple; he intimately knew the Lord. He was the one who laid his head upon the Lord's bosom during the last Passover meal (John 13:23), and the first of the disciples to recognize Him from a distance (John 21:7). And yet, John's senses were so overwhelmed by the breathtaking spectacle of believers in heaven that he humbled himself before them. Whether these individuals he saw had experienced glorification (i.e. the first resurrection) or not, we do not know, but the brilliance of their human form (whether temporary or permanent; Rev. 6:9-11), overwhelmed John's senses.

The Lord's Body

Some of what we learn about glorified bodies is presented to us in the testimonies of those who saw the Lord after His resurrection. The Lord Jesus remained on earth to encourage and instruct His disciples for forty days after His resurrection. His first appearance to them was quite a shocker. The disciples, for fear of the Jews, had gathered together in secret behind locked doors when, suddenly, the Lord stood in their midst (John 20:19). Not only could He pass through solid objects prior to His appearance, He also knew right where the disciples were. After examining the Lord's hands and His side, the disciples were completely convinced that the One before them was He that had been crucified three days earlier. This was one of five separate eye-witness accounts of the Lord on the very day He was raised from the dead. Scripture contains five more personal testimonies of the Lord's physical presence before His ascension into heaven. Paul states that on one such occasion more than 500 believers saw Him (1 Cor. 15:6).

The Lord Jesus prophesied His own resurrection (John 2:19-21; Acts 2:26-27) and showed His disciples His resurrected body (Luke 24:40; John 20:27). When He first met with the disciples after His resurrection, the Lord told them He was not a spirit, but flesh and bone (Luke 24:37-39). He then ate some fish and honeycomb in their presence (Luke 24:42). By showing the nail prints in His body to the disciples, the Lord Jesus demonstrated that the body He now had was the same body which had been nailed to a cross.

While it is true that the Lord kept some of His disciples from immediately recognizing Him after His resurrection (this was for teaching purposes), most of them clearly recognize the Lord when He appeared before them. We can therefore conclude that the Lord's glorified body was much like His pre-resurrection body in appearance, though it was flesh and bone without blood (Luke 24:39). His resurrected body could taste food, could be touched, and could be seen and heard; it also could instantly vanish and reappear elsewhere. So, while His body exhibited some properties of natural law, it also possessed supernatural qualities. Same body, but different. To illustrate this idea, I might show an old friend a picture of my son at a young age and another picture of him ten years later to highlight his growth during that time. Although it is a picture of the same person and of the same body, many features of that body have changed, while other features are similar. The Lord's resurrected body was the same one He had had previously, but it was vastly different.

When the Lord experienced resurrection, His body was changed. He still could be recognized by others, but His body was quite different than the one He possessed before. We need blood pumping throughout our bodies to stay alive, but the Lord had no blood in His body – that was shed at Calvary for you and I. The Lord's body was flesh and bone. His glorified body did not require natural metabolic operations to sustain it as our bodies do. In fact, Paul says, *"That flesh and blood cannot inherit the kingdom of God"* (1 Cor. 15:50). Obviously, the laws of existence in heaven are quite different from those our bodies on earth operate within; thus, our present bodies are not fit for heaven.

The Glorified Body

Have you ever wondered what kind of body believers will have in heaven? There were some in Paul's day that were pondering this question. Unfortunately, some of these individuals began to question the teaching of resurrection because they could not understand how a physical body could exist in heaven. Paul uses a horticultural example to explain this difficulty.

Just as a seed must fall into the ground and die in order to bring forth life, we must die to experience resurrection. Our future resurrected bodies will draw characteristics from our earthly bodies, in the same way a corn plant acquires its characteristics from the kernel of corn that was sown (1 Cor. 15:36-38). The plant is not the seed per se, but what it is, was drawn from the seed. This seems to indicate that the individuality of our human soul will be maintained in heaven, though our visible form will be quite different.

Paul says that our present bodies are perishable, weak, and are natural; however, our glorified bodies will never perish, will be powerful, and spiritual (1 Cor. 15:51-53). The former often dishonors the Lord, while that would be impossible with the lat-

31

ter body – there is no flesh nature within it to cause the glorified body to rebel against the Lord. John states that believers will have a body like the Lord Jesus' body, which obviously cannot commit sin: *"Beloved, now we are children of God; and it has not yet been revealed what we shall be, but we know that when He is revealed, we shall be like Him, for we shall see Him as He is"* (1 Jn. 3:2). Paul describes the same truth: *"For our citizenship is in heaven, from which we also eagerly wait for the Savior, the Lord Jesus Christ, who will transform our lowly body that it may be conformed to His glorious body, according to the working by which He is able even to subdue all things to Himself"* (Phil. 3:20-21). Having a Christ-like body in heaven means that everyone will morally act like God forever. There will be no ill thoughts about other people, no crippling bents, no temptations, nor will there be any addictions with which to grapple. God is a holy God and to dwell in His presence we will have to be holy too.

Paul states that the appearing of the Lord Jesus is the blessed hope of the Church (Tit. 2:11) and that those who love the Lord's appearing (i.e. live as if the Lord could come back at any moment) will be rewarded for doing so (2 Tim. 4:8). John says that those who live expectant of Christ's return will live purely, because the Lord is pure and because a believer would not want to be ashamed when He does suddenly come for His people (1 Jn. 2:28, 3:3). So although believers have not received their resurrection bodies yet, they are to live as though they have!

As the believer's flesh nature will be eradicated, the present needs and desires of our bodies will cease to exist. There will be no need for air, water, food, rest, sleep, or reproduction. The upshot is that perfect bodies will not need eyeglasses, wheelchairs, hearing aids, pacemakers, bladder napkins, dentures, hormone therapies, pain medications, sleep aids, etc. Doesn't heaven sound great?

Clothing for Heaven

Have you ever wondered how people will be attired in heaven? What will those born again in Christ be wearing? The Lord Jesus rebuked the Church at Laodicea with these words: *"You are wretched, miserable, poor, blind, and naked – I counsel you to buy from Me gold refined in the fire, that you may be rich; and white garments, that you may be clothed, that the shame of your nakedness may not be revealed; and anoint your eyes with eye salve, that you may see"* (Rev. 3:17-18). Those in the Church at Laodicea were not living for Christ; consequently, God's righteousness was not displayed in their lives. Though all believers in the Church have been positionally declared righteous in Christ, each believer has the opportunity to labor in righteousness for Christ. Those things which are done in accordance with revealed truth and in the power of the Holy Spirit have eternal value; these righteous acts are what the believer is adorned with throughout eternity. In heaven, the bride of Christ must have righteous attire; she is *"arrayed in fine linen, clean and bright, for the fine linen is the righteous acts of the saints"* (Rev. 19:8).

Paul explains in 1 Corinthians 15:40-42 that after the resurrection, some saints will shine forth the glory of God more brightly than others, just as some stars in the nighttime sky are brighter than other stars. This acquired glory directly reflects the righteous acts (good works) that are done for Christ by His strength in this present life. Eternal glory, evidently, has a weight to it; in other words, its quality is measurable (2 Cor. 4:17) and can be earned by believers through selfless service for Christ now. Thus, to be appropriately dressed for eternity, believers should secure for themselves a covering of eternal glory, which consists of righteous acts. Though saved, a believer may still appear to be spiritually naked in heaven (i.e. personal acts of righteousness on earth provide believers with varying reflections of God's glory in heaven: Rev. 3:18; 1 Cor. 15:41-42; 2 Cor. 4:17). Without being justified in Christ no one can enter into heaven and only by doing righteous acts for Him and by His power do believers contribute to their eternal attire of glory.

Though believers in heaven will reflect the glory of God in varying degrees, all the redeemed will be wearing white robes and have human form (Rev. 4:4, 19:14). Even before the martyred Tribulation saints experience glorification after the Tribulation Period (Rev. 20:4), they are described as wearing white robes in heaven (Rev. 6:11, 7:9, 13). The white robes represent divine purity and each believer's righteous position in Christ.

All will be wearing the same thing, there will be no unusual outward qualities to attract the attention of someone else, nor will we have the wherewithal to respond to such things anyway. In the book of Revelation, except for two occasions when one of the twenty-four elders speaks to John, whenever those in heaven do speak, it is in unison and to praise and worship God. One of the great blessings of heaven will be this ability to honor God corporately with one voice, which again alleviates the possibility of any believer calling attention to himself or herself.

What is delightful and precious about everyone in heaven is that they will shine forth the glory of God and desire to worship and to honor Him in everything they do. What makes heaven heaven is that the One who suffered and died for me will be there – anything that draws attention from Him will be an intolerable distraction: *"My Beloved is mine, and I am His"* (SOS 2:16).

Heaven

A young city girl was in the country for the first time and looking up into the night sky commented, "Oh, mother, if heaven is so beautiful on the wrong side, what must it be like on the right side!"[1] Indeed, how can we possibly know what God's dwelling place is like unless He tells us about it or provides us some glimpse of it? In fact, God has been providing mankind a link between heaven and earth for millennia in order to assist our understanding of His abode.

God used prophetic visions and dreams, angelic visits, and pre-incarnate appearances of the Son of God, most of which are recorded in the Old Testament, to open our understanding of heavenly things. For example, Isaiah saw a vision of God and His heavenly throne room (Isa. 6:1-8); also in a vision, Ezekiel saw the Lord, His throne, and heavenly creatures about it (Ezek. 1). Then, there are the personal testimonies of people such as Elisha, who watched his mentor Elijah ascend into heaven in a fiery chariot (2 Kgs. 2:1-11), and Moses, who, on the mount, witnessed incredible sights beyond this world, and Paul who was caught up into the third heaven (God's spiritual domain) and saw things that he could not speak of (2 Cor. 12:2-4).

John was also taken up into heaven and told to write down what he saw, but yet in some matters he was instructed not to record what he had witnessed (Rev. 4:1-2, 10:4). All this is to say that there is a good deal of biblical information which allows us to understand what God wants us to comprehend about heaven. What He has not revealed to us, we are not responsible to understand, nor is it likely that we could anyway (Deut. 29:29; Amos 4:13).

When John wrote the book of Revelation he was an old man who had been banished to the Isle of Patmos by the Roman Empire. He was spiritually caught up into heaven to preview the prophetic messages that he was to write down (Rev. 1:1, 10, 4:1-2). Paul, on the other hand, when transported into God's presence did not know whether he was in or out of his body. Yet, he was fully conscious of the Lord's presence, and allowed to see and hear most sacred things, though he was not permitted to speak of them to others. What is clear from Paul's experience, and should be an encouragement to all believers, is that though he did not know what form he was in while in heaven, he was fully aware of the Lord's presence there. This tells us that whether the believer's soul is in heaven before or after his or her resurrection occurs, the Lord's presence will be enjoyed in either case (2 Cor. 5:8; Phil. 1:23). Being with the Lord is the thrill of heaven and what all true believers long for.

What, then, does heaven look like? Much of what the Bible tells us of heaven is in metaphoric representation, so we need to be careful how we interpret the meanings of biblical symbols. Thankfully, the Bible, which was written over a 1,600 year period by about forty different writers, employs a consistent use of symbols throughout its framework. By applying the observed meanings of symbols used throughout Scripture, we can understand what God wants us to know about heaven.

Moses was to construct the tabernacle and its furnishings according to the pattern that God showed him, which was a mere shadow (an abstract copy, if you will) of the heavenly things which already existed (Heb. 8:5). John was also shown heavenly things through the use of symbolic depiction (Rev. 1:1). Besides the divine message contained in the Bible's narrative, God also uses numbers, symbols, metals, colors, names, etc. to convey information. These more abstract forms of revelation do not substitute for or supplement the clear teaching of Scripture, but rather reiterate the clear message of Scripture through metaphor. When God initially introduces an object, a number, a color, etc. in a metaphoric presentation, that symbolic meaning is held consistently throughout all sixty-six books of the Bible.

For example, let us briefly consider the subject of numerology. In Scripture, numbers one through forty are used in a consistent way when a metaphoric meaning is intended. Though most numbers in Scripture have a literal meaning, some numbers also serve a figurative purpose. The Lord Jesus, the Lamb, is described as having *seven* horns before the throne of God in Revelation 5:6. I don't believe that the Lord Jesus Christ will physically look like this in heaven. Rather, the seven horns symbolically represent His omnipotence, as *seven* is used throughout Scripture as the number of *perfection*, while a *horn* represents *power*. He is also described in the same verse as having seven eyes; as an eye represents sight, we understand this description to speak of the Lord's divine omniscience – He knows and sees all things.

The consistent use of symbols, numbers, analogies, names, first-mention occurrences, fulfilled prophetic types and shadows, plus the plain and consistent teachings of the Bible prove it to be the orchestrated genius of one Mind. It stands to reason then, that we must learn the meanings of several biblical symbols to better understand the meaning of heaven as shown to us in the book of Revelation. I will highlight some of these as we think together about heaven.

God's Throne

John was permitted to see God's throne in heaven and records what he saw in Revelation 4. In that chapter, John mentions the throne of God twelve times and is careful not to describe anything else he saw except in its relationship to the throne. To emphasize this connection, Jim Flanigan observes John's use of five prepositional clauses:

- *Upon the Throne* – Deity sitting in inscrutable splendor.
- *Round about the Throne* – a rainbow, and twenty-four crowned elders, and four strange living creatures.
- *Out of the Throne* – lightning, and thundering, and voices.
- *Before the Throne* – seven lamps of fire, a sea of glass, and the proffered crowns of the elders.
- *In the midst of the Throne* – the four living ones, who also surround the Throne; and ... the Lamb (Rev. 5).[2]

In summary, nothing is described in this heavenly scene apart from its connection with God's throne. Why? Because God is sovereign over all things and is accountable to none – everything which exists is dependent upon Him. Without God upon His throne, nothing else would matter. This is why the first sight that John describes after being caught up into heaven by the Holy Spirit was God upon His throne:

> *And He who sat there was like a jasper and a sardius stone in appearance; and there was a rainbow around the throne, in appearance like an emerald. Around the throne were twenty-four thrones, and on the thrones I saw twenty-four elders sitting, clothed in white robes; and they had crowns of gold on their heads. And from the throne proceeded lightnings, thunderings, and voices, seven lamps of fire were burning before the throne, which are the seven Spirits of God* (Rev. 4:3-5).

The priority of what John describes is important. Some think that it will be streets of gold, foundations of precious stones, and pearly gates that will make heaven special; however, heaven would not be a spectacular domain at all if God were not there. John, thus, begins his revelation with the most spectacular sight in heaven – God Himself upon His throne.

John describes the outshining of God's holy essence – His spectacular glory. The prophet relates this visible manifestation of God's essence to the colors reflected from a jasper and a sardius stone. Jasper is used twice in Revelation 21 as a symbol of God's glory in connection with the New Jerusalem, God's eternal heavenly city (Rev. 21:10-11). In fact, the walls of this city are made entirely of jasper (Rev. 21:18). Jasper is a crystalline form of silica containing fine minerals of quartz and moganite. It is neither transparent nor translucent, meaning that all visible light reaching its surface is either absorbed or reflected back to us in the colors red, yellow, brown, green, and sometimes blue. Sardius is a red stone. There is no form upon the throne to describe, only a dazzling spectacle of various hues of light emanating from it. It is noted that sardius and jasper were the first and the last precious stones, respectively, in the High Priest's breastplate (Ex. 28:17-20). These two stones mentioned in tandem, then, may be a picture of God's immutable and eternal glory.

John also saw a rainbow encircling the throne. God promised Noah that He would never destroy the earth again by water; the rainbow was given to mankind as a symbol of that covenant. The circle never stops and thus represents eternity. The compound symbol indicates that God's promises are eternal – He is a covenant-keeping God.

Around God's throne were twenty-four other thrones upon which twenty-four elders were seated. The elders represent the redeemed just resurrected from the earth, which certainly would include, but may not be limited to, the Church (Rev. 5:9). These were clothed in white raiment and were wearing gold crowns upon their heads (Rev. 4:4). These crowns, or rewards, were given by the Lord Jesus Christ to His saints for their honorable service to Him. Though there are likely many other types of crowns given to reward faithfulness, five are mentioned in Scripture:

> **The Crown of Glory** will be given to church elders who shepherd well (1 Pet. 5:4).
>
> **The Crown of Life** will be given to those who endure trials because they love the Lord (Jas. 1:12).
>
> **The Crown of Rejoicing** will be given to those who were soul-winners for Christ (1 Thess. 2:19; Phil 4:1); this crown may be more encompassing, such as a reward for spiritual growth in general.
>
> **The Crown of Righteousness** will be given to those who long for His appearing (2 Tim. 4:8).
>
> **The Incorruptible Crown** will be given to those who control fleshly desires through the Holy Spirit (1 Cor. 9:25).

The rewards that are earned during this lifetime provide the believer with a greater appreciation for the Lord, a greater capacity to worship Him throughout eternity, and indeed, a greater capability to enjoy heaven (Rev. 4:11).

As both the twelve apostles and the twelve tribes of Israel are clearly tied to the New Jerusalem in Revelation 21, it is my opinion that the same numerical representation of *twenty-four* is used here to express that all those who have been redeemed up until this point in time have experienced glorification (Rev. 5:8-10). This would include the Old Testament saints, who were mainly connected with the nation of Israel, and the Church in the

New Testament (Heb. 11:40). The Lord Jesus told His disciples that they would be seated about Him on twelve thrones in a future day, *"Assuredly I say to you, that in the regeneration, when the Son of Man sits on the throne of His glory, you who have followed Me will also sit on twelve thrones, judging the twelve tribes of Israel"* (Matt. 19:28). The scene of Revelation 4 and 5 shows that the Lord Jesus is on His Father's throne (Rev. 3:21); that is, He is still waiting to establish His kingdom on earth. At that time He will sit on His own throne in Jerusalem. The twenty-four elders on their thrones in heaven are also anticipating their opportunity to rule and reign with Christ in His kingdom.

The elders in this scene have already been rewarded for faithful service and seated in a place of honor about the throne of God and the Lamb. This event refers to the Judgment Seat of Christ, which occurs immediately after the rapture of the Church from the earth (1 Cor. 3:11-15; 2 Cor. 5:10; Rom. 14:12-14). This is a remarkable scene as humans were created to govern the world, not heaven, and humans have a lower position in creation than the angels (Gen. 1:26; Heb. 2:6-8). Yet, we never read of angels seated on thrones in Scripture, nor do they rule and reign with Christ as redeemed humanity will; they were created as eternal beings to serve God and will remain unchanged forever.

John observed that there was continual lightning, thunder, and voices proceeding out from God's throne. This description creates an unsettling disposition about the scene. We are left wondering if this ominous panorama depicts God's throne presently or relates to the future period in which John was observing it, which was just after the end of the Church Age (Rev. 4:2), and just prior to the Tribulation Period (Rev. 6:1). William Kelly answers this quandary:

> Do thunderings and lightnings and voices proceed from the throne of God at this present time? …Certainly not. The throne of God now is a throne of grace, to which we come boldly (Heb. 4:14-16). …Clearly the thunderings and lightnings and voices are the expression of God's displeasure and judicial feeling, so to speak, towards things and people upon the earth.[3]

That this scene represents the future reality of looming worldwide judgment seems to be a logical conclusion given the testimony of Scripture as a whole. Once in fellowship with God, Moses and the elders of Israel ate a meal before the Lord's throne on Mt. Sinai and all was quiet (Ex. 24:9-12). Neither Stephen nor Paul mentioned anything about thunder, lightning, and voices during their glimpses of God's throne during the Church Age. Yet, with the redeemed in heaven and on the eve of pouring out judgment on the wicked, His throne rumbles.

Before the throne are seven torches which are identified with the Spirit of God. The number seven, as earlier mentioned, is God's number and represents perfection, completeness, and holiness. The lampstand in the tabernacle and, later, the temple was patterned after this scene. Through the number seven, the light of the lampstand, (representing Christ's testimony of truth), is shown to be divine in origin. Likewise, the resource enabling the seven flames to illuminate the tabernacle, (the oil), is also shown to be divine in nature. As in Zechariah's vision of the two olive trees that supplied oil to a lampstand, the Holy Spirit is depicted in the pure oil. Speaking of the oil, the Lord told Zechariah: *"Not by might nor by power, but by My Spirit"* (Zech. 4:6). The lampstand in the tabernacle, then, speaks of God's perfect revelation of truth in Christ through the power of the Holy Spirit.

Returning to Revelation 6, the next detail John describes in relationship to God's throne is the sea of glass before it. The laver in the tabernacle and then later in the temple were patterned after this crystal sea, yet these earthly lavers held water, not glass, so a clear distinction is being made between the type and the antitype, as seen by John. Why the difference? As long as there was a Christian on earth the practical aspects of cleaning defilement from the believer's life would be a necessary ministry of Christ's intercession and Word, as pictured in the laver. But now that the Church had passed from the scene of her earthly defilement into heaven, she had no more need of the laver. The clear, ripple-free sea of glass in heaven declares that those in heaven are perfectly cleansed and at peace in God's presence. In heaven, God's people will no longer need to confess sin and obtain His cleansing – they will sin no more (1 Jn. 1:9).

Heavenly Creatures

John turns his attention from the seven flames of fire before God's throne to four spectacular creatures flying about it:

> *Before the throne there was a sea of glass, like crystal. And in the midst of the throne, and around the throne, were four living creatures full of eyes in front and in back. The first living creature was like a lion, the second living creature like a calf, the third living creature had a face like a man, and the fourth living creature was like a flying eagle. The four living creatures, each having six wings, were full of eyes around and within. And they do not rest day or night, saying: "Holy, holy, holy, Lord God Almighty, Who was and is and is to come!"* (Rev. 4:6-8).

Besides this reference to the four living creatures, the Bible informs us that there are classes of spiritual beings that exist in heaven. Besides Michael the archangel, there are cherubim (Gen. 3:24; Ezek. 1:5-14, 10:7), seraphim (Isa. 6:1-7), the four living creatures just described, and a host of innumerable angels with various functions and roles (Ps. 103:19-22). Furthermore, God describes to us what many of these spiritual beings do and how they appear before God's throne in heaven. For example, the angel Gabriel announced the births of both the Lord Jesus and John the baptizer. The four living creatures and seraphim have the occupation of flying about God's throne and praising His name, while cherubim are protectors of God's glory (i.e. they keep what is defiled from entering too close to and being consumed by divine holiness). All things recorded in Scripture have purpose, so why did God go to such effort to afford us these details? What is it that He wants us to learn?

It is my opinion that the Father is calling our attention to His Son through the appearance of these extraordinary heavenly creatures. That is, their intrinsic glories are concealed by their wings to ensure our attention remains focused on the Lamb of God, the Lord Jesus Christ. For example, the Seraphim have six wings, but only use two for flying (Isa. 6). The Cherubim were given four wings, but they also use only two for flying (Ezek. 1). God intended them to use their remaining wings to cover their own intrinsic glories while in His presence, thus assuring that only He would be adored and worshipped in heaven. Normally, these spiritual beings gladly cover themselves in God's presence, but there was a time when Lucifer, a special covering cherub, refused to cover himself and was lifted up in pride against God (Ezek. 28:13-16). He led a rebellion in heaven and likely took a third of the angels with him when he was cast out of God's presence (Isa. 14:12-15; Rev. 12:3-4, 9).

Returning to the spiritual creatures in heaven, we notice that not every part of these heavenly creatures is to be concealed with their wings; their feet, eyes, and faces are not to be covered and, in fact, should not be, for some emulated glory of Christ is being proclaimed through their visibility. So what reflects Christ's glory is seen in these creatures, but what would compete with His glory is not described – we are not to be concerned with it. This exercise of revealing God's glory and concealing competing glories in God's presence is something that the Church is to remember and practice on earth; in so doing, we pattern the holy scene now occurring in heaven (1 Cor. 11:3-16). In fact, the angels learn about submission through this practice (1 Cor. 11:10).

The scriptural accounts of the cherubim in Ezekiel 1 and 10, of the seraphim in Isaiah 6, and of the four living creatures in Revelation 4 all disclose that these beings have four kinds of faces. Apparently, the cherubim each have all four, that is, the face of a lion, the face of an ox, the face of a man, and the face of an eagle. The faces of these beings reflect the same glories of the Lord Jesus that are presented in the main themes of each Gospel. The *lion* is the king of the beasts, which reflects Matthew's perspective of Christ as king. The *ox*, a beast of burden harnessed for the rigors of serving, pictures Mark's presentation of Jesus Christ, the servant. The face of the *man* clearly agrees with Luke's prevalent theme of the Lord's humanity. Lastly, the *eagle* flies high above all the other creatures – the divine essence of the Savior is in view here, as in the epistle of John. The many eyes of the cherubim describe Christ's omniscience and their bronze feet convey His divine authority to judge the wicked in flaming vengeance (Rev. 1:15). All that the Bible describes to us about heaven, whether in structures, furnishings, or angelic beings is for the purpose of calling our attention to God's Son!

God's Eternal City

The Bible begins and ends with a wedding. Both weddings occur in a beautiful garden and in the presence of God. In Genesis 2, the first wedding is of Adam and Eve in the Garden of Eden. The last wedding in the Bible is the marriage of the Lamb and His bride before the tree of life and at the very throne of God (Rev. 20-22). Because the New Jerusalem is full of redeemed people, an angel referred to the city as the Lamb's bride while speaking to John: *"'Come, I will show you the bride, the Lamb's wife.' And he carried me away in the Spirit to a great and high mountain, and showed me the great city, the holy Jerusalem, descending out of heaven from God"* (Rev 21:9-10). Abraham knew about God's eternal city and was looking forward to seeing it (Heb. 11:10, 16). John saw this city and describes it for us:

> *He carried me away in the Spirit to a great and high mountain, and showed me the great city, the holy Jerusalem, descending out of heaven from God, having the glory of God. Her light was like a most precious stone, like a jasper stone, clear as crystal. Also she had a great and high wall with twelve gates, and twelve angels at the gates, and names written on them, which are the names of the twelve tribes of the children of Israel... Now the wall of the city had twelve foundations, and on them were the names of the twelve apostles of the Lamb. ...The city is laid out as a square; its length is as great as its breadth ...twelve thousand furlongs. Its length, breadth, and height are equal. Then he measured its wall: one hundred and forty-four cubits, according to the measure of a man, that is, of an angel. The construction of its wall was of jasper; and the city was pure gold, like clear glass. The foundations of the wall of the city were adorned with all kinds of precious stones ...The twelve gates were twelve pearls: each individual gate was of one pearl. And the street of the city was pure gold, like transparent glass* (Rev. 21:10-21).

I have visited some large cities, but this humongous heavenly city dwarfs them all. While all three dimensions of the city are

1500 miles, the height of its wall is nearly insignificant in comparison, only measuring 210 feet high (i.e. the city is 38,000 times higher than the wall encircling it). This would seem to indicate that protection of the city is not a concern, but rather the glory of it should be easily viewed by all, including those in hell.

The city has twelve foundations of precious stones and twelve pearl gates, but only one street, and it is paved with gold. In this city, no matter how one enters it, all ways lead to the city's illuminating focal point – the throne of God: *"For the Lord God Almighty and the Lamb are its temple ... for the glory of God illuminated it. The Lamb is its light"* (Rev. 21:22-23). Although the sun and moon may exist in the eternal state their light is not needed to illuminate the New Jerusalem. The Lord Jesus Christ will be its light!

God's Garden

John continues to describe the vista about God's throne: *"A pure river of water of life, clear as crystal, proceeding from the throne of God and of the Lamb. In the middle of its street, and on either side of the river, was the tree of life, which bore twelve fruits, each tree yielding its fruit every month"* (Rev. 22:1-2). Besides drinking from the pure river of water, the inhabitants of heaven are also invited to eat from the tree of life.

God calls our attention to three important trees in Scripture. The fruit from the tree of knowledge of good and evil was forbidden, but tasted by human desire (Gen. 3:1-7). The center of Scripture calls us to kneel before the suffering Savior nailed to a tree at Golgotha. Those who do are able to freely eat of the tree of life, which will be available in Heaven forever. The only remedy for sin and its handmaiden death is to obtain eternal life in Christ. Those who do will be able to eat freely from the tree of life.

After our first parents sinned, they were cast out of the Garden of Eden and prohibited from eating from the tree of life. Cherubim and a flaming sword guarded Eden to ensure every possible return route would be met with judgment – God would prevent Adam and Eve from securing humanity's eternal doom. There is only one way to the tree of life. It would be by Calvary's Road. The Lord Jesus declared, *"I am the way, the truth, and the life. No one comes to the Father except through Me* (John 14:6). That is why there is only one street in heaven leading to the tree of life. The way to God was not man venturing in, but God coming out to man. The Son of God took the judgment of the flaming sword that we might have entrance to the tree of life.

Consequently, the Bible commences and ends with the Creator in fellowship with man in a garden paradise (Rev. 22:1-6). However, the journey man travels between these two gardens is a difficult one, but thankfully this journey is bridged by a third garden – *"Now in the place where He was crucified there was a garden; and in the garden a new sepulcher."* (John 19:41; KJV). Both the first Adam and last Adam (Christ – 1 Cor. 15:45) died in a garden. The first Adam changed the first garden into a spiritual graveyard, but the Lord Jesus raised from His garden tomb to offer spiritual life. Those who receive this provision will be restored to their Creator and be returned to an eternal garden paradise. Only through the center garden of Calvary may a connection between bliss and eternity be obtained.

Conclusion

The writer of Hebrews describes the inhabitants of God's eternal city: God, His Son the Lord Jesus, angels, Old Testament believers, the Church, and, in fact, all those redeemed by the blood of Christ (Heb. 12:22-24). John affirms that no human will be able to enter through any of New Jerusalem's twelve gates unless their names are written in *The Lamb's Book of life* (Rev. 21:27). Dear reader, will you be able to enter into God's city and reside with Him forever? The Bible closes with this invitation: *"And let him who thirsts come. Whoever desires, let him take the water of life freely"* (Rev. 22:17). "Whoever will" my friend, means you; anyone desiring to satisfy his or her deep yearning to be one with God is invited to come and drink of Him. *"Oh, taste and see that the Lord is good; blessed is the man who trusts in Him!"* (Ps. 34:8).

God's Book of Names

Expecting couples often rely on a book of names to spawn ideas for naming their babies. Yet, can you imagine browsing through a book which contained every name from every culture, throughout all of time? How thick would a book of that sort be? Scripture informs us that God maintains such a record.

God's book of names is first referred to by Moses, after the Israelites had offended God by creating a golden calf and worshipping it at Mt. Sinai (Ex. 32). Moses, who had been with the Lord for forty days on the mountain, ventured down its slopes to confront the people. The calf was destroyed and 3,000 people perished that day in judgment. The next day, Moses reminded the people that they had committed a great trespass against God, and said he would return to Mount Sinai to intercede on their behalf and to learn from the Lord how atonement could be offered for their sin (Ex. 32:30-35).

Then Moses asked the Lord to blot his own name out of His book if the nation as a whole could be spared judgment. Like Paul centuries later (Rom. 9:3), he pled for God to condemn him so that mercy could be granted to the Israelites. These were hypothetical prayers, for both men knew their divine callings and that God could not condemn those He had declared righteous, but they do demonstrate the supernatural compassion of these men for their countrymen. Evidently, Moses knew that God kept a roster of the names of everyone He would create, (including those who perish in the womb), in a book entitled the *Book of the Living* (Ex. 32:32-33). David refers to this same book in Psalm 69:28, and then again in Psalm 139:15-16, which confirms that this book contains the specific details of each person prior to that individual's conception.

Moreover, Revelation 3:5 also speaks of the *Book of the Living* and assures us that the names of the faithful (true believers) are not blotted out of this book. On the other hand, unbelievers' names are blotted out of the *Book of the Living* as they die because they did not receive God's forgiveness for their sins while they were living (Heb. 9:27). This means that when it is reviewed at the Great White Throne Judgment (after the earth's destruction), it will contain only the names of the righteous. The Lord Jesus told His disciples (see Matt. 10:20) to rejoice because their names were written in heaven. The Greek verb translated *"written"* in this passage of Matthew is in the perfect tense, which means it can be rendered as Kenneth Wuest does in his expanded translation: *"your names have been written in heaven and are on permanent record up there."*[1] This statement may refer either to the *Book of the Living* or to *The Lamb's Book of Life*, which is a timeless roster of all the redeemed – all that will be saved throughout time (Rev. 21:27). Revelation 13:8 and 17:8 also speak of *The Lamb's Book of Life*. It is my opinion that the Lord was referring to this book while speaking to His disciples.

The *Book of the Living*, though written before time began, has its fulfillment in time. *The Lamb's Book of Life*, also written before creation, has its verification at the Great White Throne judgment. The former book has names blotted out of it as the lost die, while the latter remains unaltered – only the names of those who would come to salvation are written in it. Whereas the *Book of Life* (or the *Book of the Living*) initially contained the names of all those who would ever live, but those not coming to salvation never had their names written in *The Lamb's Book of Life*. Because the names of the lost, when they die, are blotted out of the former book, both books will match at the Great White Throne Judgment; their records will be in perfect agreement. The one shows God's foreknowledge, the other, His record of human responsibility.

Because of Moses' great love for God's people, he was willing to be blotted out of the *Book of the Living* in order to secure forgiveness for the Israelites. Moses was willing to suffer in the place of sinners. God's later working in human affairs would be characterized by a similar message: the Lord Jesus willingly took the place of condemned sinners at Calvary in order to secure the opportunity for them to be forgiven and restored to God.

Although Moses pictures the Lord Jesus' willingness to take the place of the condemned, Moses himself was a sinner and, therefore, could not suffer for the sins of others – he was under judgment for his own sins. Only through a righteous substitute could an unrighteous person be justified before God. Moses was not a perfect man, thus he could not be a substitute in judgment for anyone else. With this said his concern for his people is honorable and his intercession with God on the behalf of them pictures what would be perfectly accomplished through Christ in the future. Accordingly, it is only Christ's intercession and substitutional judgment at Calvary on our behalf which keeps anyone's name eternally readable in the *Book of the Living*.

Is Your Name in God's Book?

Every human ever conceived has their name written in the *Book of the Living*, whether they were born or not. The *Book of the Living* is a ledger of everyone that God has created through the process of procreation since He formed our first parents. If one dies without exercising faith in God's revealed plan of salvation, that person's name is blotted out of this book. Just believing that some higher power exists, or even in the one true God, will not save you; James warns, *"You believe that there is one God. You do well. Even the demons believe – and tremble!"* (Jas. 2:19). Clearly the demons believe in God, but are still condemned to the Lake of Fire because of their past rebellion against God (Matt. 25:41).

The Lord Jesus also made it clear that doing good works will not earn you a place in His heaven either:

> *Not everyone who says to Me, "Lord, Lord," shall enter the kingdom of heaven, but he who does the will of My Father in heaven. Many will say to Me in that day, "Lord, Lord, have we not prophesied in Your name, cast out demons in Your name, and done many wonders in Your name?" And then I will declare to them, "I never knew you; depart from Me, you who practice lawlessness!* (Matt. 7:21-23).

49

Afterlife

The Lord said many will know who He is without trusting Him as Lord and Savior. He goes on to say that many who identify with Him and do things in His name are not saved. It is quite possible for people to know a lot about the Lord and serve Him without ever being saved. The Lord knows who are truly His and who the counterfeits are.

At the Great White Throne Judgment, which occurs just prior to the Eternal State, everyone who has not experienced bodily resurrection will. Hades, the holding place of disembodied souls of the wicked, will be cleared out and these individuals, in resurrected bodies, will stand before the Lord to be judged. Some think that religion will save them and earn them an eternal place in the *Book of Life*; this will be the moment that they will learn otherwise. There are many mysterious aspects about this book, but there really is only one question which each of us should be concerned with: "Is my name written in God's registry of the redeemed?" If your name is not written in *The Lamb's Book of Life*, you will not spend eternity with God in heaven; on the contrary, you will make your eternal abode with Satan and his angels in the Lake of Fire: *"And anyone not found written in the Book of Life was cast into the lake of fire"* (Rev. 20:15).

> *He who has the Son has life; he who does not have the Son of God does not have life. These things I have written to you who believe in the name of the Son of God, that you may know that you have eternal life, and that you may continue to believe in the name of the Son of God* (1 Jn. 5:12-13).

Questions and Answers

1. Will there be individual time with the Lord in heaven?

From our space and time dependent perspective, it would seem that if there are millions of people in heaven that each person may not have access to the Lord. Certainly, much of the worship which will occur in heaven will be in unison with other believers and with various spiritual creatures (Rev. 5:11-14, 7:9-12). Yet, despite this fact, individuality among the throngs of heaven is not lost. Our need for individuality and personal recognition, however, will not be as it is now.

John tells us that every believer in heaven will be given a white stone with a special name of the Lord written on it: *"And I will give him a white stone, and on the stone a new name written which no one knows except him who receives it"* (Rev. 2:17). This action indicates that although there will be many people in heaven, each person there will enjoy a personal communion with Christ. The earthly trials that we face now tend to mold our understanding and appreciation for the Savior – He means something a bit different to each of us. In life, we develop a unique appreciation for the Savior in ways that others cannot relate to specifically; this private admiration will be cherished throughout eternity. In fact, the Lord provides us a stone with a special name on it which is befitting of our understanding of Him. No one else will know that name but the recipient of the stone; this ensures that every believer will enjoy special intimacy with the Lord, and in a way that others cannot.

2. Will there be marriages and sexual relationships in heaven?

Contrary to the Mormon and Islamic views of heaven, people in heaven will neither be male nor female, at least in the way we understand the genders to exist today. There will be no marriages or sexual relationships in heaven as these, and other world religions, tout. The Lord confirmed this truth while responding to a fictitious scenario posed by the Sadducees, a religious sect which formed part of the Jewish judicial court called the Sanhedrin. The Sadducees did not believe in the supernatural, and thus mocked the doctrine of resurrection. They asked the Lord Jesus about a woman who had been married to seven different men (she was widowed seven times and never married to more than one man at once): *"In the resurrection, whose wife of the seven will she be? For they all had her"* (Matt. 22:28). Rather that preaching to them again a message they had already rejected the Lord used the opportunity to affirm the truth of resurrection:

> *You are mistaken, not knowing the Scriptures nor the power of God. For in the resurrection they neither marry nor are given in marriage, but are like angels of God in heaven. But concerning the resurrection of the dead, have you not read what was spoken to you by God, saying, 'I am the God of Abraham, the God of Isaac, and the God of Jacob'? God is not the God of the dead, but of the living* (Matt. 22:29-32)

Those who experience resurrection will not be gender-significant. They will be like the angels, who are neither men nor women, although when they present themselves in human form to deliver God's messages, they have always appeared as men. For example, in Genesis 18, Abraham prepared a meal for three wayfaring men, who were later revealed as the Lord and two of His angels. Although it was not necessary for their own sustenance to do so, these three spiritual beings enjoyed fellowship with Abraham and Sarah and ate the meal that they had prepared for them (Gen. 18:8). As the Lord demonstrated after his resurrection, the consumption of food is still a possibility, though certainly not a necessity, for a glorified body. Apparently, angels can partake of food if the situation requires them to (Gen 19:3).

Male and female genders were God's design to provide complementing companionship in marriage and for the purpose of procreation (Gen. 1:28, 2:18). In heaven, the need for reproduction will be eliminated – everyone will be eternal. Moreover, our communion with God in heaven will far exceed anything we could have ever experienced in an earthly relationship. Accordingly, we will be completely satisfied with being in fellowship with God and desire nothing else, including marital relationships. One of the clear warning signs of a false teaching is the notion that fleshly desires will be satisfied in heaven, or even worse, that such things are a part of some supreme deity's reward system.

We are a three-part being: spirit, soul, and body, and God wants to control all of us (1 Thess. 5:23). That goal will be achieved once believers have received their glorified bodies. In heaven, our human spirit, (i.e. our inner man that is God-conscious), will perfectly control our soul, (which composes our will, emotions, personality, and mental faculties). Our human spirit will be under the full control of the Holy Spirit, which will ensure deep satisfaction with God and that we will not covet any cheap substitutes at the flesh level.

3. What will we do in Heaven?

Unfortunately, many people have the impression that heaven will either consist of people sitting on puffy clouds while strumming their golden harps, or else engaging in the things they most enjoyed doing on earth. While the book of Revelation does mention that saints will sing and play harps, this is not for entertainment purposes, but rather is their contribution to the corporate worship of God (Rev. 5:8, 15:2). The redeemed will have the ability to sing and praise God with one voice. If you are hoping that there will be fishing, golfing, bowling, hunting, scrapbooking, knitting, etc. in heaven, I'm sorry to disappoint you, but there won't be. But be encouraged: if heaven is your final destination, you will not desire these activities anymore anyway.

Besides worshipping the Lord, the redeemed will rule and reign with Christ over the nations during His Millennial Kingdom on earth (2 Tim. 2:12; Rev. 4:4, 20:4). During this time all the curses that were placed upon the earth as a result of human sin will be removed (Rom. 8:19-22). Those individuals who do not take the mark of the beast and live through the Tribulation Period will repopulate the earth during the Kingdom Age; the rest of the people on earth at Christ's second coming will be destroyed with the Antichrist and False Prophet (Matt. 25:31-41; Rev. 19:20-21). During this entire 1,000 year period, Satan and his angels will be confined to the bottomless pit (Rev. 20:1-3).

As mentioned previously, at the end of the Kingdom Age, Satan will be loosened from his prison and will attempt to deceive as many people as possible to rebel against the Lord. His goal will be to take as many people as possible to the Lake of Fire with him. Satan and the demons know their end (Luke 4:33-35; Matt. 25:41); their defeat certain, they content themselves with keeping people from worshipping God. At the Great White Throne judgment, all of the wicked, including the angels, will be judged by Christ, and also believers will take part in that judgment process (1 Cor. 6:3). The believer has a bright future in Christ. Besides the opportunity to praise and worship the Lord with unhindered affections and unfailing strength, the believer also rules and reigns with Christ, judges the wicked with Christ, and inherits all things with Christ (Rev. 21:7). Being with Christ ensures that heaven will be a wonderful place to spend eternity.

4. Will we recognize others in heaven?

Martin Luther, the night before he died, was reasonably well, and sat with his friends at a table. The matter of their discourse was whether or not we shall know one another in heaven. Luther held the affirmative position, and this was one reason he gave: Adam, as soon as he saw Eve, knew what she was, not by discourse, but by divine revelation; so shall we know others in the life to come.[1]

Scripturally speaking, the rich man suffering in Hades knew who Abraham and Lazarus were and who his brothers (still living) were. David said that he would see his deceased infant son again after death (2 Sam. 12:23). Those in Revelation who had been martyred during the Tribulation Period and had gone to heaven were fully cognizant of what had happened to them and requested that God take vengeance on their oppressors (Rev. 6:9-11). The disciples, though a bit confused at first, recognized the Lord Jesus after His resurrection (Luke 24:31; John 20:20).

Apparently, death does not prohibit us from recognizing loved ones, even if they have not yet experienced resurrection – we intuitively know their spiritual essence. There must, then, be the ability of individuals to distinguish other souls even when there is not a body; thus, it would stand to reason that individuals after experiencing resurrection would still be discernable (i.e. the resurrected body would contain the same soul that was recognized before). As explained earlier, the resurrected body draws characteristic from its mortal body (1 Cor. 15:37-39), which allows it to be similar in appearance to its previous earthly form. The resurrected body will represent God's best design for that individual; perhaps this is the reason that when angels appear in human form, they never appear as children or as elderly.

5. Will there be babies in heaven?

The short answer to this question is yes and no. I do not believe that we will see half-pint glorified people rollerblading down heaven's gold pavement. Each one there will be God's best impression of who he or she is and all will have the opportunity to see the Lord without requiring a stool or step-ladder. Nowhere in Scripture do we read of a heavenly nursery for departed babies or of children roaming about heaven. With that said, it is my opinion that those who die before understanding the moral law within them (Rom. 2:15), and God's solution for sin will be there in the same type of full-sized bodies that everyone else will have. These souls would not be part of the Church, but would nevertheless be trophies of God's grace.

In Adam, we all died (Rom. 5:12), so no matter how cute a baby is, he or she was born in sin (Ps. 51:5). This is why the Lord Jesus said, *"He who believes in Him is not condemned; but he who does not believe is condemned **already**, because he has not believed in the name of the only begotten Son of God"* (John 3:18). We all have been conceived and born into sin. Thus, a holy God would be just in condemning all rebels to the Lake of Fire; naturally speaking, we are all born as enemies of God (Rom. 5:6-10). But the Lord has a solution to this situation: *"But God, who is rich in mercy, because of His great love with which He loved us, even when we were dead in trespasses, made us* *alive together with Christ (by grace you have been saved)"* (Eph 2:4-5). God can legitimately make such an offer because He judged His own Son for all of our sins – Christ took our place in death and judgment (Hebrews 2:9). Those who accept this offer are *"not condemned,"* and those who reject it are *"condemned already"* (John 3:18).

God has a great concern for children, and threatens those who abuse them with dire consequences (Matt. 18:6). Children have guardian angels to provide a certain level of protection against the forces of evil which work to prevent them from understanding divine truth and turning to God (Matt. 18:10). Just as a shepherd with one hundred sheep is concerned about one lamb that strays from the fold, God is concerned about each child and desires that none be lost (Matt. 18:14).

But what about those people who have never had an opportunity to either accept or reject God's offer of salvation, (i.e. embryos, newborns, the mentally disabled, etc.)? In other words, what about individuals who died before they were morally conscious and consequently did not hear of God's solution to their sin problem? There is not enough Scripture addressing this matter to make a conclusive statement, but the above conclusion, (that these people will be granted a place in heaven), seems consistent with God's gracious character as demonstrated in similar situations. For example, those under twenty years of age were not judged with the older Israelites who had doubted and murmured against the Lord at Kadesh-barnea (Num. 14:29-33). As previously mentioned, David certainly believed that he would someday see his deceased newborn son in heaven (2 Sam. 12:23). There is one thing that we can be sure of in this matter: *"Shall not the Judge of all the earth do right?"* (Gen. 18:25). Yes, God will do what is right!

Your Afterlife Adventure

Before embarking on a long journey, it is wise to obtain a road map to ensure you will find the desired destination. Life itself is a long spiritual journey and, likewise, we need a map of the way. Many spend significant time planning a family vacation or a sightseeing trip, but neglect to properly prepare for their afterlife. Thankfully, God has given us the Bible, His spiritual map to resolve the matter of sin and guide us safely into eternity. Left to ourselves, we would never know God personally because we would never know how to seek after Him.

After our first parents sinned, spiritual death (separation from God) passed down to all their descendants (Rom. 5:12). That is why Scripture states that an individual is already condemned even before he or she might reject the gospel message of Jesus Christ (John 3:18). Paul summarizes our natural spiritual condition by saying, *"There is none righteous ... none who seeks after God"* (Rom. 3:10). In our natural state, man is hopelessly lost and separated from God as a result of sin.

The Matter of Sin

Sin is not a popular word. It describes "lawlessness," "rebellion," "not doing what we know is right," "falling short of God's standard of righteousness" (Rom. 3:23; James 4:17). God's moral standard of right and wrong is declared to man in the Ten Commandments. These commandments show us our sin (Rom. 3:20) and affirm that we need a Savior (Gal. 3:24).

The first two of the Ten Commandments relate to the subject of recognizing God as Creator and not worshipping creation: *"You shall have no other gods before Me"* (Ex. 20:3); *"You shall not make for yourself any carved image"* [anything that is worshipped or adored more than God] (Ex. 20:4). We are each commanded to love and serve God above all else. These commandments alone are sufficient to prove that each of us has sinned against God, but in case you are not convinced, here is a paraphrased summary of the remaining commandments (Ex. 20:3-17):

- Do not blaspheme God or use His name disrespectfully.
- Put aside one day in seven to honor the Lord.
- Honor your parents.
- Do not murder.
- Do not commit adultery.
- Do not steal.
- Do not lie.
- Do not covet (lust after what is not yours).

If you ask people on the street if they are a good person, most will say, "Yes, I am a pretty good person." Their moral standard of reckoning, however, is all wrong and they don't even know it. They have fabricated a self-righteous system of weighing their good deeds against their bad (sin), thinking that their good deeds will somehow offset their sins. God's standard of judgment is quite different – absolute perfection! By His standard, one sin will keep anyone out of heaven (Gal. 3:10-12). Someday each of us will be judged by God's standard of perfection (Eccl. 12:14; Rom. 14:10-12; Rev. 20:11-15).

How do you measure up against His standard of impeccable holiness? The Bible answers that question for us on two counts. First, as to the matter of sin, *"All have sinned and fall short of the glory of God"* (Rom. 3:23). Secondly, as to good works, *"All our righteousnesses are like filthy rags"* (Isa 64:6). So, one sin will tip God's moral scales against us because good works cannot satisfy God's righteous demand that our sins must be punished.

Imagine for a moment that you are driving a car faster than the posted speed limit and, appropriately, are pulled over by a highway patrolman. While he is writing you a citation for speeding, you boast to the patrolman that you are a good parent and a good spouse, that you do community service work, that you give generously to charities, etc. To your frustration, the patrolman continues writing and hands you the citation – you are fined $250. What is the moral of the story? No amount of good works undoes the fact that we all have violated God's moral law. Yet, through the doings of humanized religion man attempts to convince himself that he does not deserve God's judgment. Water baptism, good works, religious parents, church attendance, tithing, repetitious prayers, rubbing beads, reciting religious chants, etc. cannot undo the consequences of violating God's standard of righteous. We have all transgressed God's holy standard and because He is a holy God, He must judge our sin!

In our natural state apart from God, our good works do absolutely nothing to earn God's favor. The flesh nature opposes God in deed and motive; therefore, there is nothing inherent within the flesh that can please God to earn salvation. Jeremiah states, *"The heart [seat of emotion] is deceitful above all things, and desperately wicked"* (Jer. 17:9). The grand conclusion is that we all are sinners and that we can do nothing to persuade God to love us more than He already does. While good works are evidence of true salvation in Christ, they cannot be the basis for salvation (Jas. 2:17, 20).

The Consequence of Sin

How then can man obtain a pure standing with God? The answer is that each individual must be justified, that is, declared right by God. This is how Abraham received salvation: *"Abraham believed God, and it was accounted to him for righteousness"* (Rom. 4:3). If anyone could have merited salvation through personal effort, it would have been Abraham, but Scripture indicates he would have been condemned if he had not received the righteousness of God by faith. Justification is an accounting term which means "to impute or accredit to another's account." When an individual trusts Christ, God imputes a righteous standing to that individual's account (he or she is declared righteous before God, though in practice he or she will still sin). This reality is a positional truth which the Christian is to practically live out on a daily basis (Rom. 6:11-12, 13:14).

Afterlife

If you die without being justified, (i.e. receiving forgiveness of your sins and obtaining a righteous standing in Christ), there is no hope for you (Heb. 9:27). Contrary to what some teach, there is no purgatory – you will spend eternity in hell. Christ has already done everything necessary to purge you of your sins (Heb. 1:3), and rescue you from eternal judgment, but He will not force you to go to heaven – it is your choice (2 Pet. 3:9). The Bible vividly describes the ultimate fate of those who reject God's truth. The following are terms used in association with hell:

- *"Shame and everlasting contempt"* (Dan. 12:2)
- *"Everlasting punishment"* (Matt. 25:46)
- *"Weeping and gnashing of teeth"* (Matt. 24:51)
- *"Unquenchable fire"* (Luke 3:17)
- *"Indignation and wrath, tribulation and anguish"* (Rom. 2:8-9)
- *"Their worm does not die* [putrid endless agony]*"* (Mark 9:44)
- *"Everlasting destruction"* (2 Thess. 1:9)
- *"Eternal fire ... the blackness of darkness forever"* (Jude 7, 13)
- *"Fire is not quenched"* (Mark 9:46)

Revelation 14:10-11 tells us the final, eternal destiny of the sinner: *"He shall be tormented with fire and brimstone ... the smoke of their torment ascended up forever and ever: and they have no rest day or night."* The Bible's teaching of eternal punishment for unforgiven sinners offends people; consequently, many are watering down the truth, teaching that hell is a state of non-existence or quick annihilation. However, misrepresenting the truth to avoid its consequence is never a good idea.

God does not enjoy punishing rebels, but His character demands it. He longs for all men to repent and to turn to Him by faith, as He has said, *"I have no pleasure in the death of the wicked, but that the wicked turn from his way and live"* (Ezek. 33:11). Everlasting "hell fire" was not originally prepared for mankind but, rather, for Satan and other rebellious angels (Matt. 25:41). However, God will use this place of torment to also punish those who reject His only solution for sin – the substitutionary death of His Son.

God will not force anyone against his or her will to receive Christ so that they might live with Him in heaven. Heaven would be hell if you didn't want to be there, but hell will not be a heaven for those rejecting Christ. Salvation is like a personal check that has been written out for the full value of our offenses against God, which God extends to us in the person of Christ. As an individual believes on Christ, he or she is, by faith, endorsing the check and the value of it is imputed to their personal account. The check has value whether we cash it or not, but it only has value in our account if by faith we take action to cash it. God will not force your signature – the choice is yours.

The Solution to Sin

The Lord Jesus said, *"Unless you repent you will all likewise perish"* (Luke 13:3). Repentance means that you agree with God that you are a sinner deserving His judgment and that you first turn away from all you thought would earn you heaven; such repentance indicates a deep grief over personal sin and a desire to turn from wickedness (Jer. 8:6). Secondly, you must turn *to* something – that is, you must believe the gospel of Jesus Christ. To alleviate any confusion about what this message is, the Lord Jesus Christ personally conveyed it to Paul, who then wrote: *"Christ died for our sins according to the Scriptures, and that He was buried, and that He rose again the third day according to the Scriptures"* (1 Cor. 15:3-4). Believing any other gospel results in eternal damnation (Gal. 1:6-9).

If by faith one believes and receives Christ for the forgiveness of his or her sins, he or she is then spiritually born again (John 3:3; 1 Pet. 1:23) and becomes an adopted child of God (Rom. 8:15-16). Both in earthly families and in God's family, birth and adoption are acts which establish *relationship*. However, as a child of God our *fellowship* with Him is not secured through relationship alone, it depends on our righteous behavior (1 Jn. 1:5-10). Ongoing godly behavior is only possible through the abiding presence of the Holy Spirit; if the believer chooses to obey revealed truth, his or her fellowship with God is unbroken. If one sins, fellowship is broken, but the relationship remains, for it is secured in Christ. As Christians sincerely confess their sins they are fully restored with God (1 Jn. 1:9).

The Lord Jesus said the way to eternal life is found only in the narrow way (Himself), but the path to destruction is wide: there are many ways leading into hell (Matt. 7:13-14). The Lord went on to say only a few would find the narrow way and the narrow gate which leads into the eternal bliss of heaven.

When we enter the narrow way by trusting the gospel message of Jesus Christ, God rewards us with Christ and all the riches that are in Him (Eph. 1:3). By God's mercy, the believer escapes hell, and by His grace, he or she inherits heaven and all that Christ has (Rev. 21:7). Will you not trust Christ for salvation and know the wonder of God? The Lord Jesus is both the beginning and the end of man's spiritual journey! If you hear His pleading voice, please don't harden your heart; trust the Lord Jesus Christ for the salvation of your soul.

> *For God so loved the world that He gave His only begotten Son, that whoever believes in Him should not perish but have everlasting life. For God did not send His Son into the world to condemn the world, but that the world through Him might be saved. He who believes in Him is not condemned; but he who does not believe is condemned already, because he has not believed in the name of the only begotten Son of God* (John 3:16-18).

Concerning one's spiritual journey into the afterlife, individuals have limited choices: to ignore the supernatural altogether, to have a "make me feel good" rapport with religion, or to have an intimate relationship with God through the Lord Jesus Christ. The reader must decide what is the more pertinent, reliable, and genuine path in life to follow. If you decide that knowing God is more crucial than an intellectual link with science or the "guilt-numbing" remedy of religion, you must approach God through Christ alone; there is no other way to be saved. Speaking of Jesus Christ, Peter said: *"Nor is there salvation in any other, for there is no other name under heaven given among men by which we must be saved"* (Acts 4:12). How will you venture into eternity?

Endnotes

Preface

1. P. L. Tan, *Encyclopedia of 7700 illustrations* (Bible Communications, Garland TX; 1996, c1979); death

The Basis of Understanding

1. Edythe Draper, *Draper's Quotations from the Christian World* (Tyndale House Publishers Inc., Wheaton, IL), # 9867
2. Ibid.; "Christianity"
3. P. L. Tan, *Encyclopedia of 7700 Illustrations* (Bible Communications, Garland TX; 1996), #5397 "Only Two Religions"
4. Edythe Draper, op. cit.; "Christianity"

Facing Death

1. P. L. Tan, op. cit., 1025
2. W. Grinton Berry ed., *Foxe's Book of Martyrs* (Power Books, Old Tappan, NJ; no date), p. 9
3. Thomas Aquinas, quoted by Nancy Gibbs, "The Message of Miracles" *Time* (New York, NY; April 10, 1995), Vol. 145, No. 15, p. 68
4. http://www.actsweb.org/articles/article.php?i=6&d=1&c=1&p=1
5. P. L. Tan, op. cit., 16
6. F. W. Krummacher, *The Suffering Savior* (Baker, Grand Rapids, MI: 1977), p. 111
7. http://www.christian-faith.com/forjesus/words-of-dying-atheists-and-skeptics
8. http://www.biblebb.com/files/MAC/sg2141.htm
9. http://www.christian-faith.com/forjesus/words-of-dying-atheists-and-skeptics
10. P. L. Tan, op. cit., 1039
11. Ibid., 1046
12. Ibid., 1040
13. http://www.christianchronicle.org/article1985550~Bonhoeffer_continues_to_warn_against_godless_piety

Three Deaths and One Life
1.   Edythe Draper, op. cit.

Resurrected Bodies
1.   P. L. Tan, op. cit., 2195

Heaven
1.   P. L. Tan, op. cit., 2197
2.   Jim Flanigan, *Notes on Revelation* (Gospel Tract Publications; 1987), pp. 40-41
2.   Ibid., 2196
3.   William Kelly, *The Elders in Heaven*, http://www.stempublishing.com/authors/kelly/7subjcts/eldershv.html

God's Book of Names
1.   Kenneth S. Wuest, *The New Testament: An Expanded Translation* (Eerdmans Pub. Co., Grand Rapids, MI; 1989), Matthew 10:20

Questions and Answers
1.   P. L. Tan, op. cit., 2196

Acknowledgements

The author appreciates all those who contributed to the publishing of *Afterlife*. Special thanks to Mike Attwood and David Dunlap for editorial contributions. Thanks also to Kathleen Henderson for general editing and David Lindstrom for proofreading assistance, and to Ben Bredaweg for cover design.

ORDERING INFORMATION:

Case quantities of *Afterlife* may be purchased for $1.25/book through Gospel Folio Press. Individual copies may be obtained from Gospel Folio Press or various internet book-retailers.

Gospel Folio Press
Phone: 1-800-952-2382
Website: order@gospelfolio.com